STARK COUNTY DISTRICT LIBRARY

W9-BWT-440

DISCARDED

HUMPBACK WHALE
MIGRATION

BY L. E. CARMICHAEL

The Child's World®

Published by The Child's World®
1980 Lookout Drive • Mankato, MN 56003-1705
800-599-READ • www.childsworld.com

ACKNOWLEDGMENTS
The Child's World®: Mary Berendes, Publishing Director
Content Consultant: Dr. Tanya Dewey,
    University of Michigan Museum of Zoology
The Design Lab: Design and production
Red Line Editorial: Editorial direction

PHOTO CREDITS
Pavel Losevsky/Dreamstime, cover (top), 1, back cover; Melissa Fiene/
Dreamstime, cover (bottom), 2-3; Josh Friedman/iStockphoto, 4-5; The
Design Lab, 6-7; Earle Keatley/iStockphoto, 8; Anne Connor/iStockphoto,
9; Night and Day Images/iStockphoto, 10-11; Witold Kaszkin/Dreamstime,
12-13; Barb Malc/iStockphoto, 14-15; Konrad Mostert/iStockphoto,
16-17; Oleg Podzorov/Fotolia, 19; Evgeniya Lazareva/iStockphoto, 20;
Dale Walsh/iStockphoto, 21; Jan Kratochvila/iStockphoto, 22-23; Fins 'n'
Flukes/Fotolia, 24; Oksana Perkins/Fotolia, 27; Lisa Combs/Fotolia, 28; Sam
Chadwick/Shutterstock Images, 29

Design elements: Pavel Losevsky/Dreamstime

Copyright © 2012 by The Child's World®
All rights reserved. No part of this book may be reproduced or utilized in
any form or by any means without written permission from the publisher.

ISBN 9781609736224
LCCN 2011940065

Printed in the United States of America

**ABOUT THE AUTHOR: Lindsey
E. Carmichael earned a PhD
for studying the migration
of wolves and arctic foxes
in Canada's North. Now she
writes nonfiction for children
and contributes to the science
blog, Sci/Why. Lindsey lives in
Nova Scotia, which is a summer
feeding area for North Atlantic
humpback whales.**

TABLE OF CONTENTS

HUMPBACK WHALES

Whales swim in the ocean, but they are not fish. Whales are **mammals**. Like all mammals, they breathe air. They have live babies. Whale mothers feed their babies with milk. And whales have hair.

Humpback whales live in every ocean. But they are not always in the same place. They feed in polar oceans in the Arctic and the Antarctic. They have their babies in tropical oceans near the equator. Humpbacks swim long distances through the ocean.

The humpback whale's lifetime journey is its migration. This is when an animal moves from one **habitat** to another. Migrations happen for many reasons. Some animals move to be in warmer weather where there is more food. There they can reproduce, or have their babies. And these migrations can be short distances, such as from a mountaintop to its valley. Or they can be long distances, like the humpback's ocean journey.

*Humpback whales
are mammals.*

MIGRATION MAP

Humpback whales have a **reproductive** and **seasonal** migration. Humpback whales that feed in the north Pacific Ocean near Russia go to Japan to calve. Whales from Alaska calve around Mexico or Hawaii. Humpback whales around Canada calve in the Caribbean. The whales from Greenland or Norway usually travel to northwestern Africa to calve.

Whales from the southern **hemisphere** feed near Antarctica. These whales migrate to several different places. Some travel to Costa Rica in Central America or Brazil in South America. Others calve near southwest Africa, Madagascar, Australia, or New Zealand. There is also a group of humpback whales that may not migrate. This group is in the Indian Ocean.

This map shows the migration routes of humpback whales around the world.

PACIFIC

OCEAN

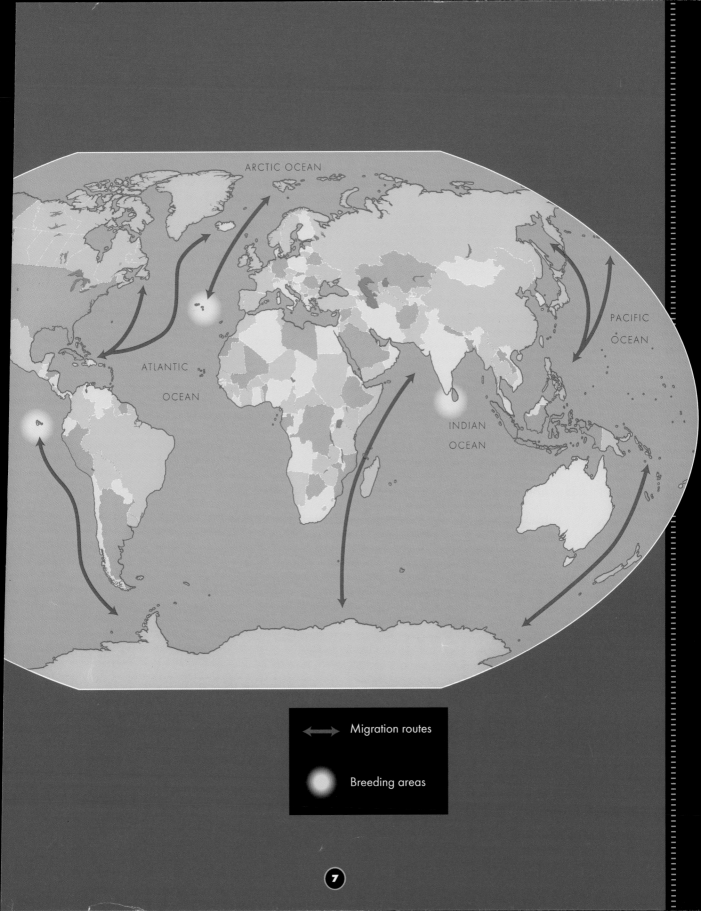

ARCTIC OCEAN

PACIFIC OCEAN

ATLANTIC OCEAN

INDIAN OCEAN

Migration routes

Breeding areas

WONDERFUL WHALES

There are two types of whales. They are toothed whales and baleen whales. Toothed whales include dolphins, sperm whales, and killer whales. Baleen whales include blue whales, fin whales, and humpback whales. Humpback whales do not have teeth. They have baleen. Baleen is made of **keratin**. This is the same material that is in fingernails. Baleen forms a screen in the whales' mouths.

Humpback whales often stay near the coast. This makes it easy for people to spot them. Female humpbacks are called cows. Male humpbacks are called bulls. A humpback's flippers are one-third its body length. The humpback has the longest flippers of any whale.

Most of the time, humpbacks swim near the coast.

SUMMER IN THE ARCTIC

It is summer. In the North Pacific Ocean near Alaska, a humpback whale is feeding. The whale swims in a slow spiral around a school of fish. It starts deeper and moves up toward the surface. As it swims, it breathes out through the blowhole on top of its head. This lets out a ribbon of bubbles.

The fish pack closer and closer together. The bubbles look like a wall around them. The fish feel trapped inside. The humpback swims through the fish with its mouth open. It takes a big gulp. The whale pushes the water out through its baleen with its tongue. The fish are trapped inside the humpback's mouth. Then the humpback swallows.

A humpback opens its mouth and takes a big gulp of fish and water.

This is how the humpback hunts. It is called bubble netting. The humpback is the only type of whale that does this. Different humpback **populations** make different kinds of nets. In the North Atlantic Ocean, a group of whales blow clouds of bubbles instead. Sometimes humpbacks hunt in groups. The humpback is the only baleen whale that does so.

Humpbacks sometimes feed in groups.

A HUMPBACK WHALE
EATS 1 TO 1.5 TONS
(0.9 TO 1.3 TONNES)
OF FOOD EACH DAY.

In the polar oceans, the surface water gets very cold in the winter. Cold water is heavier than warm water. The surface water sinks to the bottom of the ocean. Water at the bottom gets pushed up to the surface. This is called **upwelling**.

Upwelling brings **nutrients** from the ocean bottom to the surface. Tiny plants called algae use these nutrients and the sun's energy to grow. The algae become food for millions of **krill**. Krill are food for fish. Krill and small fish are both food for humpbacks.

In the North Pacific, humpbacks feast from June until September. A single whale might gain as much as 10 tons (9 tonnes) of blubber in just four months. Blubber is a thick layer of fat under the whale's skin. It keeps whales warm in cold polar oceans.

Blubber is also used as a food source. Humpbacks need to store a lot of energy in their bodies. That is because they will not eat for the next eight months. They will be making a long journey. It will take them to tropical waters. Unlike polar oceans, tropical waters stay the same temperature all year round. That means upwelling cannot happen. Tropical oceans have much less food for whales than polar oceans.

Upwelling causes algae to grow in cold waters.

*A humpback baby
is born at the
calving grounds.*

THE CALVING GROUNDS

Silver Bank is a calving ground for humpback whales. It is in the Caribbean Sea, off the coast of the Dominican Republic. Thousands of humpback whales visit this area. Some scientists believe that half of the whales in the North Atlantic are born here.

Pregnant cows stay at their feeding areas as long as they can. They are usually the last to arrive at the calving grounds. Most cows have their babies between January and February. A humpback calf is a big baby! It can be about 13 feet (4 m) long. It weighs up to 3,000 pounds (1,361 kg) at birth.

As soon as the calf is born, its mother pushes it to the surface. The calf takes its first breath of air. Then the calf is ready to nurse. Humpback whale milk is very fatty. This helps the calf grow as quickly as possible. The calf also uses milk fat to make blubber. The blubber keeps the calf warm during its first migration to the feeding area.

Female humpback whales come to calving areas for two reasons. One is to give birth. The other is to choose a mate. Normally the cows that mate are ones that do not have young calves.

Scientists believe male humpbacks have two ways to attract females. First, bulls fight with other bulls to prove that they are strong. They jump out of the water, or **breach**. They hit the water with their flippers. Then they charge each other. They push and shove other males. Sometimes these fights are just for show. Sometimes the whales are hurt, though.

Male humpback whales are known for their singing. Their songs are made up of moans, trills, and gurgles. Humpbacks have the most complex songs of any type of whale. One song can last up to 20 minutes. Males sing their songs over and over. Some songs last many hours. Bulls sing at different times and in different places. Scientists do not know for sure what these songs mean. But male humpbacks often sing at calving areas. Their song might be the second way bulls attract mates.

After mating, female humpbacks migrate back to their feeding areas. A humpback may take three months to get from its calving area to its feeding area. Pregnant cows want to start eating as quickly as possible. While her baby grows inside her, the cow needs lots of energy. A female humpback is pregnant for about 11 months. She will not give birth until she returns to the calving area next year.

A bull breaches as one way to find a mate.

A LONG SWIM

Humpbacks make the longest journeys of any mammal. People noticed humpback whales in different places at different times of year. That meant that humpbacks migrated. No one knew, however, which paths humpbacks took. Scientists have answered this question using photographs. Humpbacks have black and white patterns on their flukes. These patterns do not change. They are unique to each whale, similar to a human's fingerprints.

When whales come to the surface, scientists take photos of their flukes. The photos are stored in huge collections. Each new photo is compared to all the other humpback photos. If a certain whale's picture is taken in two different places, that whale has migrated. Then scientists can figure out which path the whale took.

Each humpback has a unique pattern on its fluke.

THE MAMMAL MIGRATION
RECORD IS HELD BY A BULL
HUMPBACK WHALE. HE
TRAVELED FROM ANTARCTICA
TO SAMOA AND BACK. THAT
IS A DISTANCE OF MORE THAN
11,700 MILES (18,840 KM)!

WHY MIGRATE?

Once scientists knew where the whales were going, they could start to figure out why. Some scientists believe humpbacks migrate to protect their calves from **predators**. Killer whales live near humpback feeding areas. These predators cannot kill adult humpbacks. Instead, they attack the smaller baby whales. Tropical oceans are a safer place for calves to be born. Killer whales do not live there.

Other scientists have a different idea. When humpback whale calves are born, they do not have blubber. It would be very hard for newborns to stay warm if they were born in cold polar waters. Calving areas have warmer water. In these places, whale calves do not have to use the energy from milk to stay warm. All the milk they drink can be used for growing and making blubber.

Killer whales eat humpback calves.

FINDING THEIR WAY

Many humpbacks use the same feeding and calving areas every year. Others visit different areas in different years. Sometimes, whales choose not to migrate at all. These whales stay at their feeding sites year round.

Whales that do migrate seem to know exactly where to go. Some humpbacks migrate along coastlines. They stay close enough to shore so that they can see the land. Once in a while, whales stick their heads above the water. This is called **spyhopping**. Scientists thought whales might be looking for landmarks. If they saw something they recognized, the humpbacks would know where they were.

Spyhopping may be a way for humpbacks to see where they are going.

Many humpbacks migrate through the deep ocean. They are too far away to see land. The whales cannot see landmarks on the bottom of the ocean, either. Humpbacks must have another way to find their route. Some clues whales could use include ocean currents, water temperature, stars, or the angle of the sun. Scientists discovered that humpbacks have a special material in their brains. It is like a compass in the whales' heads. It allows whales to sense the earth's natural magnetic field. This is a force in the earth. It is what makes a compass needle point north.

To find out which clues humpbacks use, scientists did a study on the whales. They put devices on 16 humpback whales. The devices tracked where the whales swam. Scientists could see where the whales were at all times. They followed the humpbacks from 2003 to 2010. The devices showed that humpbacks swim in straight lines.

The whales in this study migrated from different places and took different paths. That means that each whale felt different parts of the earth's magnetic field. When their migrations were over, three of the whales arrived in the same area. The scientists decided that humpbacks have a migration map in their heads. But we still do not know how that map works.

Humpbacks somehow know the right direction to swim.

Humpback whales were widely hunted for a century.

HUNTING HUMPBACKS

Whales of all kinds were hunted in great numbers between 1860 and 1966. Humpbacks were killed by **whalers**. Humpbacks are often found near coastlines. That made them easier to catch. Humpbacks have a lot of blubber for a whale their size. Whale blubber is a solid fat. People used it to make oil. Whale oil was used in lamps, to grease machines, and to make margarine. Other parts of whales were also used. Whale meat became food for people and animals. Baleen was made into hair brushes. Whale bones were added to ladies' clothing. Whale bones could also be ground into powder and used as in the soil to help plants grow.

Scientists do not know how many humpbacks were killed by whalers. Some think 100,000 died. Others believe more were killed. By 1960, humpback whales were in danger of going **extinct**. In 1966, it became illegal for most people in the world to kill humpbacks. Some native people can still kill humpbacks, though. And scientists can kill humpbacks for scientific research.

Scientists have been trying to find out how many humpbacks are left. They count them using the same photographs that are used to study whale migrations. Scientists believe more than 60,000 humpbacks are alive today.

NEW DANGERS

Humpback populations have been getting bigger since whaling was outlawed. That is good news. But humans have other ways of putting whales in danger. Many ships sail the oceans. If ships hit whales, the whales can be injured or even die. Whales also get tangled up in fishing nets.

Humans are also making big changes to the oceans. One way is through **climate** change. Gases made from cars and factories are trapped in the air. It makes Earth's temperatures rise. This affects the whales' food supply. If the water gets too warm, algae and krill may move to new locations. That would change the location of feeding grounds. Warmer temperatures could decrease the humpbacks' food supply. Climate change may also stop upwelling from happening.

Pollution is another way humans change the oceans. On purpose or by accident, humans pour dangerous **chemicals** into oceans. We also put chemicals on soil. When it rains, water runs off the soil and carries the chemicals into rivers. Eventually, the rivers reach the ocean.

Big ships can hit and hurt humpback whales.

The amount of pollution in ocean water might be small. But algae are tiny plants. Algae absorb chemicals from the ocean. When krill eat the algae, they also eat the chemicals. Fish eat the chemicals in the krill. Humpbacks then eat the chemicals in the fish. With every step in the food chain, the amount of pollution in the animals gets bigger and bigger.

BETWEEN 1999 AND 2003, BOATS KILLED SEVEN NORTH ATLANTIC HUMPBACKS. IN THAT TIME, 13 OTHER WHALES DIED BECAUSE THEY GOT TANGLED IN NETS AND DROWNED.

Many of the worst chemicals get trapped in the whales' blubber. That is bad news for baby whales. Humpback mothers do not eat while they nurse their calves. They make milk using the fat in their blubber. The whale calf eats the pollution from the blubber when it nurses. The pollution could harm the way the baby whale grows. It might make it harder for the calf to have babies of its own some day. Scientists do not know what pollution will do to humpbacks, but they are worried.

Another new worry is noise pollution. People sail in ships, dig into the ocean bottom, and use **sonar** to look for submarines. This makes a lot of noise that was never in the ocean before. Whales use sounds to find each other, to find mates, and to talk to each other. Extra noise could keep them from doing these things. More whales are also getting stranded. When a whale is stranded, it swims too close to land. It ends up on a beach and dies. A whale can lose too much moisture, be crushed by its weight, or drown when the tide comes in. Many strandings happen in areas that are very noisy. Some stranded whales appear to have hearing problems. That could mean that noise pollution hurts migration, too.

Sound pollution may cause humpbacks to beach themselves.

As long as humpbacks can still migrate, they may be able to survive changes to their habitat. Humpbacks can travel long distances. They can cross entire oceans. They might even be able to find new feeding and calving areas if old ones are destroyed. With luck, whale watchers will see humpbacks swimming, bubble hunting, and spyhopping for many years to come.

People watch the humpback whale's migration from boats.

TYPES OF MIGRATION

Different animals migrate for different reasons. Some move because of the climate. Some travel to find food or a mate. Here are the different types of animal migration:

Seasonal migration: This type of migration happens when the seasons change. Most animals migrate for this reason. Other types of migration, such as altitudinal and latitudinal, may also include seasonal migration.

Latitudinal migration: When animals travel north and south, it is called latitudinal migration. Doing so allows animals to change the climate where they live.

Altitudinal migration: This migration happens when animals move up and down mountains. In summer, animals can live higher on a mountain. During the cold winter, they move down to lower and warmer spots.

Reproductive migration: Sometimes animals move to have their babies. This migration may keep the babies safer when they are born. Or babies may need a certain habitat to live in after birth.

Nomadic migration: Animals may wander from place to place to find food in this type of migration.

Complete migration: This type of migration happens when animals are finished mating in an area. Then almost all of the animals leave the area. They may travel more than 15,000 miles (25,000 km) to spend winters in a warmer area.

Partial migration: When some, but not all, animals of one type move away from their mating area, it is partial migration. This is the most common type of migration.

Irruptive migration: This type of migration may happen one year, but not the next. It may include some or all of a type of animal. And the animal group may travel short or long distances.

SOMETIMES ANIMALS NEVER COME BACK TO A PLACE WHERE THEY ONCE LIVED. THIS CAN HAPPEN WHEN HUMANS OR NATURE DESTROY THEIR HABITAT. FOOD, WATER, OR SHELTER MAY BECOME HARD TO FIND. OR A GROUP OF ANIMALS MAY BECOME TOO LARGE FOR AN AREA. THEN THEY MUST MOVE TO FIND FOOD.

GLOSSARY

breach (BREECH): To breech is to break through something, such as the water's surface. Humpbacks breach to find mates.

chemicals (KEM-uh-kuhlz): Chemicals are materials made using chemistry. Chemicals cause pollution in the ocean.

climate (KLYE-mit): The climate is the usual weather in a place. Climate change may affect humpback whales.

extinct (ek-STINGKT): A type of animal is extinct if it has died out. Humpbacks are in danger of becoming extinct.

habitat (HAB-uh-tat): A habitat is a place that has the food, water, and shelter an animal needs to survive. The polar oceans are the summer habitat of humpbacks.

hemisphere (HEM-uhss-fihr): A hemisphere is one half of the earth. Some humpbacks live in the southern hemisphere.

keratin (CARE-uh-tin): Keratin is a protein found in horns, hair, human fingernails, and other things. Baleen is made from keratin.

krill (KRIL): A krill is a small animal that is like a shrimp. Krill are food for humpback whales.

mammals (MAM-uhlz): Mammals are warm-blooded animals whose females make milk for their young. Humpback whales are mammals.

nutrients (NOO-tree-untz): Nutrients are things that people, animals, and plants need to stay alive. Upwelling makes nutrients rise to the surface of the ocean.

populations (pop-yuh-LAY-shuhnz): Populations are the animals of one type that live in the same area. Different humpback populations migrate to different areas.

predators (PRED-uh-turs): Predators are animals that hunt and eat other animals. Killer whales are predators of humpback calves.

reproductive (ree-pruh-DUHK-tiv): Reproductive is something related to having babies. Humpback whales have a reproductive migration.

seasonal (SEE-zuhn-uhl): Seasonal is something related to the seasons of the year. Humpback whales swim long distances on their seasonal migration.

sonar (SOH-nar): Sonar is a method of sending sound waves into the water to find where something is in the water. Sonar may hurt humpback whales.

spyhopping (spye-hop-PING): Spyhopping is when humpback whales stick their heads straight out of the water to look around. Spyhopping may help humpbacks find their way in the ocean.

upwelling (UP-well-ing): An upwelling is when seawater rises from the bottom to the top. Upwelling is important to the humpback's food source.

whalers (WAY-lurz): Whalers are people who hunt whales for their meat, oil, and bones. Whalers once killed many humpback whales.

3 1333 04042 0422

FURTHER INFORMATION

Books

Catt, Thessaly. *Migrating with the Humpback Whale*. New York: PowerKids Press, 2011.

Douglas, Lloyd G. *Humpback Whales*. New York: Children's Press, 2005.

Hirschmann, Kristine. *Humpback Whales*. San Diego: Kidhaven Press, 2003.

Jenner, Caryn. *Journey of a Humpback Whale*. New York: Dorling Kindersley, 2002.

Web Links

Visit our Web site for links about humpback whale migration: *childsworld.com/links*

Note to Parents, Teachers, and Librarians: We routinely verify our Web links to make sure they are safe and active sites. So encourage your readers to check them out!

INDEX